Unlocking the Dawn: Mastering The 5 AM Lifestyle,Own Your Morning And Your Path to Success

Jose R. Johnson

INTRODUCTION

Unlocking the 5AM Club's Potential
Time is our most valuable resource, and how we
spend it may make or break our personal and

professional life. In the business world, where competition is tough and expectations are constant, mastering time management might be the key to success. Enter the 5AM Club, a game-changing concept with the ability to change the way you approach your day and your goals.

The 5AM Club is not a closed, member-only club, nor is it a complicated secret society. It's a simple and powerful concept that anyone can grasp: getting up at 5 a.m.can be the impetus for a life-altering transformation.
We will explore the significant benefits of joining this self-created club in this book, tearing down the hurdles to entrance and accompanying you on a path to unleash the immense power that early mornings may give.

The Benefit of Getting Up Early

Imagine waking up to a peaceful, uninterrupted period of time all to yourself. A time when the rest of the world is still sleeping and the distractions of daily life are at their lowest. This is what the 5AM Club provides: uninterrupted, quality time to focus on your personal development, profession, and overall well-being.

The 5 a.m. start time is not about sacrificing sleep or becoming a slave to the alarm clock. It is all about developing a conscious and intentional daily routine that will set you up for success. It is about taking control of your day before external events do.

Finding extra hours in the day can seem unattainable in our fast-paced society, when the demands of work, family, and personal life seem never-ending. This is where the 5AM Club comes in, providing an organized and effective way to devote valuable time to self-improvement and goal achievement.

The Road Ahead

In this book, we will delve deep into the concept of the 5AM Club and investigate the numerous ways it can effect your life, notably in the realms of business and profession. We'll talk about the power of early mornings, the science behind them, and how you can use this time to hone your abilities, increase your productivity, and reach your full potential.

We will also offer practical tactics and insights into creating a morning routine that is in line with your goals. From creating a morning ritual to effectively managing your time, you will discover how to make the most of your early start.

But the 5AM Club is about more than simply personal development; it's about creating a disciplined, resilient, and focused mindset. These qualities are crucial in the corporate sector, where difficulties and rivalry are constant. By joining the 5AM Club, you will receive a competitive advantage that will set you apart from your colleagues and help you ascend to the top.

Workplace 5AM Club

Early mornings are hardly a novel concept. Many great people throughout history, from Benjamin Franklin to Richard Branson, have stood by the advantages of getting up early. The 5AM Club concept has gained popularity among entrepreneurs, professionals, and high achievers in recent years. They understand that the first few hours of the day are a gold mine of opportunity, a period when they may concentrate on what actually counts.

The 5AM Club mentality can be game changer in the workplace. It can assist you in prioritizing work, making sound decisions, and increasing your productivity. You'll have made great progress toward your goals by the time others are just getting started. We'll look at how to apply the 5AM Club concepts at work, whether you're a business owner, manager, or employee.

A Path to Harmony

While the 5AM Club values productivity and performance, it also recognizes the value of balance. It's not about working too hard or trying to burn the candle at both ends. It's about making the most of your early morning hours to work productively, freeing up time for leisure, family time, and self-care.

In the pages that follow, we'll look at ways to live a balanced life while pursuing your professional goals. We'll talk about the role of health and wellbeing, the importance of disconnecting from work, and the value of excellent connections. The 5AM Club promotes achievement in all facets of life, not just business.

Your Own 5 a.m. Club

This book will help you create your own 5AM Club that is suited to your specific requirements and goals. You'll find actionable ways to harness the power of early mornings in a way that works for you, whether you're an early riser or a lifelong night owl.

By the end of this trip, you will have the knowledge and inspiration to embrace the 5AM Club and realize its revolutionary potential. You'll learn how to make early mornings a habit, how to use them to promote your profession, and how to live a healthy and satisfying life.

Are you ready to tap into the power of the 5AM Club and begin on a journey of personal and professional development? Let us go on this transformative adventure together.

CHAPTER 1:

Getting Up Early: Your First Step Towards Success

What is the one habit that every successful person in the world, regardless of occupation, practices? Getting up early in the morning is that habit. Getting up early invigorates and inspires you to get moving. It takes discipline to get up early every day, and discipline is one of the most critical qualities required for significant success. Waking up even when you are fatigued requires pushing yourself beyond your limits, which is another crucial trait for success. There are countless examples of ultra-achievers waking up while the rest of the world sleeps:

If you have no intention of getting up early, disregard and skip this post. However, if you've been considering getting up early, this post is for you. Here, I'll walk you through the steps you can take to start waking up earlier.

1. Establish a goal. When do you want to get up?

"What time do I want to wake up?" ask yourself.

It's too ambiguous to tell yourself to get up early without a definite time. If waking up is difficult for you, a vague remark like that is doomed to fail.

Setting a goal also serves as a wake-up call. If you normally get up at 10 a.m., getting up at 5 a.m. will be difficult, if not impossible. Instead, start small and pick a reasonable goal.

2. Make a purpose for yourself to get out of bed early.

After you've established your goal, the following stage is to figure out why you want to get up early in the first place.

I've mentioned a few advantages of getting up early. And it's better if you can figure out why you want to do that for yourself. It might be to

Do some work before your children get up.

Before you leave for work, go to the gym.

Plan your day before other people's agendas take over.

Being clear about the cause makes it simpler to get up early or, at the very least, not click the snooze button and fall back asleep.

3. Begin by going to bed earlier.

It is now time to take action. One of the biggest reasons why most individuals can't get out of bed early is because they sleep too late at night.

Let's be honest here. You must go to bed early if you want to wake up early.
 Getting up early by sacrificing valuable sleep is not a long-term strategy. It also contradicts your goals of waking up early because you are unlikely to feel refreshed when you get out of bed.

As a result, make sure you get adequate sleep every day. On average, most people will need 7 to 9 hours of sleep per night.

4. Improve your sleep quality by optimizing your sleep.

Aside from sleeping earlier, adjusting your sleep environment will also help you sleep better.

Make your bedroom dark and quiet to increase the creation of the sleep hormone melatonin, which will knock you out.

At the same time, maintain a cool room temperature of 16 to 20 degrees Celsius (60 to 70 degrees Fahrenheit).

5. Establish a bedtime routine.

In episode 8 of Work Less, I discussed the importance of having a morning and evening routine. A pre-bedtime ritual will help you get to bed earlier and increase your sleep quality significantly.

Wind down for 60 to 90 minutes before bed. I normally begin my nightly ritual with a 10-minute daily review. Then I read for 20 to 40 minutes before going to bed.

You can also increase your sleep quality by doing the following:

Caffeine should be avoided. 8 to 10 hours before bedtime, with breakfast 2 hours before bedtime.

Completely disconnect from your work and personal duties.

Avoid high-intensity exercises that raise your body temperature.

Reduce or, better yet, avoid blue light exposure before going to bed. In other words, no screen time before bed.

6. Getting up early

Now that you've finished preparing for sleep, it's time to go to bed and get up early the next day.

Use an alarm clock, particularly during the first one to two weeks. A sleep monitoring alarm to wake you up during your light sleep phase would be beneficial. If you don't have a sleep tracking alarm, the 90-minute rule from Richard Wiseman's book Night School may come in handy.

A whole sleep cycle (light sleep, deep sleep, and REM) normally takes about 90 minutes. Set your alarm by dividing your sleep period into 90-minute increments.

7. Incorporate the habit into weekends and special occasions.

Now that we've covered the basics of how to get up early, let's move on to weekends and special events.

You may have other weekend plans. However, sticking to a steady sleep schedule may make it much easier in the long run. If you need to sleep later than normal on weekends, try to keep the change in sleep time to one to two hours.

Prepare and plan ahead of time for important events such as vacations and conferences. This may appear severe, but if you're serious about waking up early, schedule your work and personal life around your sleep.

In other words, prioritize your sleep.

Master your sleep to get up early.

You don't have to get up early to be productive and successful. Waking up at 5 a.m. does not suddenly transform someone into a high performance.

As you may have seen, all of the preceding processes are intimately tied to sleep. Finally, it comes down to how you safeguard your sleep and manage your energy to make the most of your waking hours.

To summarize, remember that altering your behavior takes time. Instead of rushing to achieve your objective (waking up early), track and measure your progress and focus on taking tiny steps at a sustainable pace.

Morning Routine: A Productivity Roadmap

The world is run by routines.

The most important step in reaching personal greatness is developing, adopting, and mastering your own routine.

Every decision you make throughout the day depletes your body's energy; the best method to save that mental energy is to automate as many decisions as possible through the use of routines. When you aren't wasting valuable mental energy deciding what to do next, you may devote it to deep work.

Let's take a look at how I've helped busy professionals and entrepreneurs create a routine that saves their mental energy for vital work rather than the everyday grind.

Building a solid daily routine is more important than ever in the digital age. A daily routine can assist you in prioritizing your time, increasing productivity, decreasing stress, and achieving your goals.

The following are the stages to creating a successful daily routine that works for you.

Step 1: Determine Your Priorities

Identifying your priorities is the first step in creating an effective daily routine. This entails taking some time to consider what is most important to you. Consider your short- and long-term objectives, personal values, and the things that give you the most joy and fulfillment. Make a list of your top priorities using this information.

It's critical to discern between achievable and unrealistic goals. Doable priorities are things that are essential to you but also practically feasible in your current situation. Unrealistic priorities, on the other hand, are things that are essential to you but are either impossible to achieve in your current situation or demand considerable adjustments to your lifestyle.

Assume you have a demanding work schedule and a family to care for. Spending quality time with your family, taking care of your health through exercise and eating well, and remaining on top of your professional tasks are all realistic objectives. Your unrealistic priorities could include traveling the world for a year or starting a side business.

You can begin to develop a daily routine that matches with your doable priorities by recognizing them. For example, you could set time each day for family activities, exercise, and job responsibilities that must be performed. You may ensure that your daily routine is meaningful and purposeful by focusing on these priorities.

It's also worth noting that your priorities may shift over time. For instance, if you go through a major life event or transition, such as having a child or starting a new career, your priorities may adjust to accommodate these changes. In this instance, you should reconsider your priorities and adapt your daily schedule accordingly.

Step 2: Plan Your Day

After you've determined your priorities, it's time to plan your day. This entails developing a daily schedule that includes time for work, rest, and play. Begin by scheduling time for your most critical activities, such as work or exercise. Then, fill the balance of your day with activities that are related to your priorities. Make time for rest and relaxation.

Routines in the morning.

A good morning routine is essential for organizing your day. How you begin your day is a powerful predictor of how your day will progress. Exercise, reflection, and learning should all be part of your morning routine for the best benefits. This doesn't have to be long: a 15-minute stroll, ten minutes of gratitude journaling or meditation, and ten minutes of reading.

Begin small and realistically.

When developing a daily regimen, it is critical to start simple and be realistic. Trying to change your entire schedule all at once might be stressful and unsustainable. Instead, begin with tiny modifications and gradually progress to a more regimented schedule. Be realistic about how much you can get done in a day and be open to change your schedule as needed.

Accept Flexibility

Unexpected incidents and disruptions are unavoidable, no matter how meticulously you arrange your daily routine. It is critical to be adaptable and open to adjust your routine in response to changes in your schedule or unforeseen circumstances. Accepting flexibility can assist you in remaining calm and focused in the face of unforeseen problems.

Step 3: Maintain Your Routine

It's one thing to create an effective daily regimen; it's quite another to keep to it. It is critical to develop a regimen that is both sustainable and reasonable for your lifestyle. If you're having trouble sticking to your schedule, consider changing it as needed. It's also critical to be adaptable and willing to adjust your routine in response to unforeseen events or changes in your schedule.

Discover Your Flow

When it comes to productivity and creativity, everyone has a particular natural rhythm. While some people like working late at night, others would rather work early in the morning.
Pay attention to your natural cycles and schedule your most important work at your most productive times. This allows you to accomplish more in less time and feel more fulfilled throughout the day.

Share your routine with a friend or family member, and ask them to contact you on a regular basis to see how you're doing. Having someone hold you accountable for your actions can be a powerful incentive.

Track how many days you have done your habits in a row using a calendar or a Google Sheets spreadsheet. Create a streak that you don't want to break.

Remove Distractions.

Identify any potential distractions, such as social media or television, that may hinder you from sticking to your plan and identify strategies to eliminate them from your daily routine.

Your phone is one of the most typical causes of distraction.
When possible, leave it outside of your office or work space and watch your productivity increase.

Step 4: Monitor Your Progress

It is critical to track your development to verify that your daily habit is beneficial to you. This might assist you in identifying areas where you may need to make changes or enhance your habits. Consider keeping a journal or utilizing an app to keep track of your daily activities and goals.

I made a Google spreadsheet to track my progress and assign myself points for completing targets. If you incorporate your tracking mechanism into your routine, this might provide as an additional layer of accountability.

Consider your progress. Write on what you think is working well or poorly. During your morning reflection, write about it. It's amazing how many solutions you may find when you reflect on both your happy and bad days.

Celebrate Your Success

Creating an effective daily routine is a journey rather than a destination. It's critical to appreciate your tiny victories along the way.

Take time to celebrate your accomplishments and view failures as opportunities to learn and improve.

Step 5: Schedule time for self-care.

In addition to making time for work and other activities, it is critical to include self-care in your daily routine. This includes activities such as exercise, meditation, and spending time with family and friends. Self-care can help you recharge your batteries and reduce stress, allowing you to be more productive and focused.

It is practically hard to endure for long periods of time when your body, soul, and intellect are neglected. Don't sacrifice your health for success. Self-care is crucial because, in order to live a happy life, you must expect a lot from your body, which involves properly caring for it and giving it what it needs, even if it is not the easiest option to make.

Creating a good daily routine is a necessary step toward personal greatness. It will require time and work, but the rewards will be well worth it. You may create a routine that works for you by establishing your priorities, structuring your day, accepting flexibility, creating accountability, and avoiding distractions.

Remember to track your progress on a frequent basis to ensure that your program is effective. A effective daily routine can provide tremendous benefits such as more time for what matters, better productivity, decreased stress, and progress toward your goals.

Consider the following question when you create your daily routine: What are your top three priorities in life, and how can you create a daily routine that coincides with those priorities?

Remember to be realistic, adaptable, and ready to change your routine as needed. You may create an effective daily routine that supports your personal and professional progress with focus and perseverance.

So, what are you holding out for? Begin developing your world-class regimen right away!

CHAPTER 2 :

Effective Time Management

Time management is one of the most beneficial abilities that will propel you forward in your personal and professional life. You'll eventually find yourself in a chaotic situation if you don't manage your time well.

Time, as such an important component of existence, deserves to be treated with the utmost respect. The only way we can improve our lives is by being proficient in the art of time management.

To seize control of every minute of your life, you must understand what successful time management is and how to manage time.

What exactly is time management?

The synchronization of tasks and activities to maximize the effectiveness of an individual's efforts is referred to as time management. Essentially, time management allows people to complete more and better work in less time.

What is the significance of time management?

Learning the art of time management may have a positive impact, particularly Thus, the following are some benefits it offers:

. improved task management

. Increased output

. There are no stress levels.

. Improved work-life balance

On the other, if you are unable to efficiently manage your time, you may face the following negative consequences:

. Deadlines were missed.

. Work of poor quality

. Stress levels that are higher

. Work-life balance

. Result in burnout

Employees can simply manage their hours to the best effect with smart time management. When things go as planned, people are more creative, happier, and less likely to burn out at work. As a result, it makes sense to set aside some time to learn about time management ideas and techniques that will assist your career.

Some people appear to have enough time to complete whatever they desire, but others are constantly switching from one to task. This merely indicates that the individual makes every effort to optimize their time and cultivate effective time management techniques.

Time management skills are a collection of abilities that aid in time management.

Among the abilities are:

. Keeping organized

. Prioritizing what you need to get done

. Setting specific objectives

. Excellent communication abilities

. Planning the day efficiently

. **Practicing task delegation**

. **Positively dealing with stress**

What can I do to enhance my time management abilities?

Now that you understand the significance of time management, you must put these strong time management techniques into action.

15 time management tips for work to help you reach your objectives:

1. Get up early – Extend your day.

We all have 24 hours in a day. Though you cannot modify the number of hours in a day, you might attempt waking up a little earlier to make your day longer than others. To function optimally, your body requires 6-8 hours of sleep per night.

Begin by setting your alarm 15 minutes earlier than usual and gradually extend the time frame. This extra time can be used to exercise, meditate, prioritize, or even pursue a hobby. Gradually, your everyday productivity will grow, and time management will no longer be an issue.

2. Set SMART objectives – Don't simply wish, do.

Do you realize there is a correct and incorrect approach to set goals? When your goals are not being met, something is wrong with your strategy. However, if you set goals correctly, your productivity might skyrocket.

Set S.M.A.R.T. goals: Specific, Measurable, Achievable, Realistic, and Time-bound. These objectives would provide structure to your professional life and prepare you for what lies ahead.

3. Look for time tracking software -

Using time management software is one of the simplest ways to keep track of every minute spent at work. These time tracking programs are intended to help you make time estimates, measure time spent on activities, and keep a record of every minute you spend working on assignments.

If you are working on a project, for example, you can set a time estimate for each job and subtask to better manage your time. You can use time management software such as ProofHub to efficiently manage your tasks and time.

ProofHub's Time Tracking Function:

ProofHub is one solution for time tracking and management. It is a time tracking software that consolidates all of your time data into a single location. What are your options?

.Timesheets should be added.

To record time data, multiple timesheets can be added, which can then be used for payroll, client billing, tracking, and even time management.

.Make time estimations.
Setting time estimates is a useful technique to manage time since you can determine how long it should take to complete tasks. If the time taken exceeds the predicted time, you will be notified.

.Time is manually tracked.
You can enter time taken to complete tasks and manually track time spent for billable or non-billable hours.

.Use many timers to keep track of time.
Start and pause timers as you switch between tasks and save them in timesheets.

.With the assistance of timesheets
Acquaint yourself with accurately recording your time, using timesheets to your advantage,

and embracing all of the various insightful data that a time tracking software has to offer.

.Timesheets can be exported.
Export timesheets for use in client billing, payroll, and time management.

.Timesheets should be saved.
Archive timesheets from the time section for future use.

.Timekeeping reports
To see tracked hours, create custom time reports all in one tracking application.

"With time management software, you can better plan and prioritize your time." Check out ProofHub."

4. Mornings should be reserved for MITs – the most vital jobs.

Mark Twain once remarked, "Eat a live frog every morning, and nothing worse will happen to you for the rest of the day." His point is to tackle the most critical work first thing in the morning. If you have two or more frogs to eat, start with the largest one.

Prioritization and time management go hand in hand. You can only efficiently manage your time if you know what needs to be done when. The goal is to take on a difficult or time-consuming work, do it, and then move on to other things.

5. Find your comfort zone.

You've probably observed that at certain times of the day, you're as concentrated as an eagle and your productivity skyrockets. It occurs when your mind is completely in sync with the external circumstances. Some refer to it as "flow," while others refer to it as their "zone."

Discovering your flow or zone might help you use your time more effectively. It assists you in reaching an optimal state of awareness, which allows you to feel and perform at your best.

6. Distracts should be avoided at all costs.

Among the most common and important office distractions are emails, phone calls, and social media messages. So much so that you waste 759 hours per year as a result of workplace diversions. A task that ought to take 60 minutes takes longer than three hours to finish because of numerous interruptions.

Put your phone on silent mode and turn off data if you are working on high-priority chores. You would ultimately become more efficient and save a great deal of time.

7. No multitasking — Priority is given to quality over quantity

If you take satisfaction in juggling too many chores at once, we have some bad news for you. According to one study, only 2% of adults can multitask efficiently. For the remaining 98% of folks, multitasking actually wastes time and reduces overall productivity.

Instead of dividing your attention among three distinct objects, concentrate totally on one and marvel at it. Try timeboxing them to make it more effective. It refers to the act of assigning a time range to each activity, which increases the possibility of its completion.

8. Take frequent short breaks to replenish and renew.

Breaks may seem paradoxical, but they are one of the most successful time management tools. How? Let us consider two scenarios. Think about the first situation, when a team member puts in five to seven hours a day at work. In addition, a different team member is working on the same task with brief pauses in between.

Who, in your opinion, is using his time the most effectively?
Obviously, the latter.

Smart time management does not necessarily entail doing one thing or another. It also emphasizes how taking brief breaks every hour or so can greatly increase productivity.

9. Find motivation through quotes, videos, and audiobooks.

Following a to-do list or a set pattern might be tedious. When you're not totally motivated at work, it's difficult to concentrate. Instead than wasting time doing something useless, use it to inspire yourself.

Tape cliched time-management quotes all over your desk. Listen to audiobooks or watch motivational or TEDx videos about time management at work. Or just take a short stroll.

We've all heard of the procrastination phenomenon, in which you either do nothing or indulge in pointless things. Chronic procrastinators get a strange high when they postpone crucial tasks for later, and when it is too late, they panic. Don't let procrastination take over your life and become a way of life for you.

The most effective technique to deal with procrastination is to divide your job into several tasks. It not only makes it feasible, but it also provides a starting place from which to begin work. Make precise schedules that offer you an exact notion of deadlines as well. When you surround yourself with people who take action and crush targets quickly, you will naturally adopt such habits and become more proactive at work.

10. Aim for 7-8 hours of sleep each night.

Sleep is a negative component that can have an impact on many things, both favorably and adversely. Sleeping for six to eight hours not only makes you feel refreshed and renewed, but it also helps to a healthy lifestyle. On the contrary, not getting enough sleep increases your risk of developing diseases such as diabetes, obstructive sleep apnea, obesity, and others.

When the human mind and body are well-rested, they make better decisions and function more efficiently. You can swiftly select what to do, when to do it, and how to accomplish it. Create a sleep schedule and stick to it every day. Try going to bed and getting out of bed at the same time. There are numerous applications, such as Calm and Sleep Cycle, that track your sleeping patterns, assist you in getting a good night's sleep, and wake you up as a more focused individual.

11. Do fewer but more significant things

Taking on more than you can handle is never a good idea. Around the world, high achievers and exceptional performers do less but better. When you prioritize tasks, you gain clarity and direction, allowing you to begin working on things, save time, and be more productive.

When you're having trouble managing your time, take a deep breath and focus on one task at a time, completing it before beginning another.

12. Make use of an online calendar.

Using an online calendar is one of the best time management ideas for managers. Calendars have long been used as a basic time management tool. With the development of online calendars, it is now possible to quickly manage one's schedule, mark important dates and activities, set reminders, establish time blocks, and so on.

The best aspect is that online calendars may be integrated with third-party apps and accessible from a variety of devices. There are numerous options to choose from, such as Google Calendar, Outlook Calendar, and Apple Calendar, but the ProofHub project calendar simplifies the way you manage your schedule, plan your events, and keep track of the important dates and deliverables in the project, allowing you to always stay ahead of the deadlines.

ProofHub calendar has the following additional features:

. Add recurring events and tasks – If a task must be completed on a regular basis, you can arrange any event or task to recur without having to recreate it.

.Configure automated reminders — Configure automatic reminders for events or tasks.

.Set the calendar display to day, week, two weeks, or even a month.

.Create secret milestones and events – By making a task or event private, you can limit its exposure to only yourself.

.Calendars can be downloaded in PDF, CSV, or iCal formats.

13. Organize comparable tasks together

Little things like grouping comparable chores together might also save you a lot of time. We are all aware that different activities necessitate different forms of thought and planning. Instead than bouncing from one work to the next randomly, it would be wise to group them together.

For example, rather than answering essential business emails and phone calls throughout the day, you can set up a certain time to do so. It allows you to structure your work and time priorities. Furthermore, concentrating on related things allows your brain to focus better and complete tasks from your list more quickly. Managing recurring chores and events in advance can save you a lot of time and work.

14. Outsource or delegate

You don't have to do everything as a beginner, executive, or manager. One of the most beneficial aspects of delegating and outsourcing is that it allows you to focus on more important tasks while significantly reducing your workload. No matter where you are in your professional career, learning how to delegate responsibilities to others and share the load with others is always a wise decision.

Pro tip: To transcribe meeting notes and phone calls, many busy professionals use services like Rev.com. Not only is a record of the call useful, but it's also a wonderful tool to elicit more insights from talks and rapidly share summaries with teammates who might benefit from the information.

If you find it difficult to delegate work or devote time to training people for certain duties, you may always outsource or employ a freelancer. Both delegating and outsourcing, when done effectively, may be significant time savers for you and your organization.

15. Keep track of your time.

To better manage time at work, you must understand how and where each hour is spent. Begin manually or with a time tracking tool tracking your time. People that want to keep track of their activities tend to be focused, productive, and organized. They keep track of not just the number of hours they work but also the number of actions they complete, jobs and projects they handle, and clients they work for.

ProofHub is a popular time-tracking program used by NASA, Taco Bell, and Disney to log hours and keep organized. The online time management system enables you to make time estimates, measure time spent on tasks, and obtain minute-by-minute details, allowing you to manage time efficiently and bill clients accurately utilizing time data.

Pro tip: To measure and visualize email activity and productivity, many busy professionals use programs like Email Analytics. It's a useful tool for keeping track of how much time you spend on email, whether with clients, vendors, prospects, or colleagues.

Techniques for Time Management

With the aforementioned work time management tips in hand, it's time to move on to outstanding time management tactics that will turn you into a time management pro. Using time management techniques is not about cramming a lot of chores into your day, but rather about simplifying how you operate in order to do things effectively. You'll have more time to do the things you enjoy if you use smart time management skills. Because we believe in the philosophy of "working smarter, not harder," time management is essential.

"Time management is not a supplementary activity or skill." It is the foundational skill upon which everything else in life is built."

Let's look at some well-known and extensively utilized time management techniques:

1. The rule of 80/20

The 80/20 concept, often known as the Pareto principle, states that 80% of outcomes result from 20% of acts or efforts.

This signifies, according to Investopedia:

The product line's 20 goods account for 80% of sales volume.

80% of a company's revenue is generated by 20% of its clients.

80% of a company's output is generated by 20% of its personnel.

Pareto's principle maintains time management at the forefront by allowing you to focus on the most critical tasks rather than wasting time on chores that won't make a difference.

For example, it is preferable to read 10 articles in an hour (glancing over for a little more than 5 minutes) and choose two finest ones in the next hour than to spend two hours reading three articles in depth.

It may be challenging at first, but after you're acclimated to it, you'll notice an increase in productivity and be able to better manage time and effort.

2. The ABCDE procedure

If you're having trouble managing and spending your time effectively, try using the ABCDE approach to define priorities. Here's how to apply the preceding strategy as a time management tip for both work and personal purposes.

In this method, you first create a list of chores and then categorize each task as A, B, C, D, or E, in which:

A indicates for the most vital duties: You must finish these activities at all costs or face catastrophic consequences.

. B denotes less significant chores: These actions should be completed but will not have the same impact as those listed above.

. C stands for chores with no consequences: These are tasks that would be great to complete but have no repercussions whether you accomplish them or not.

. D stands for tasks for delegate: If something may be assigned to someone else, it is marked as

D. It could, however, be situational because not every duty can be delegated to someone.

. E indicates chores that can be eliminated: An E task is something absolutely useless that may be deleted because it isn't already benefiting your productivity and efficiency.

3. The four-dimensional system

Do you know what the four Ds are for time management?

These four D's stand for DELETE, **DELEGATE, DEFER**, and DO. Let us go over them quickly:

Delete (Drop): There will always be things that do not require your attention and can be removed from your list.

Delegate: If someone can do something even 75% better than you, delegate it to them. If you don't have anybody to assign work to, you can either start teaching him or outsource the task.

Defer: Not everything should be done right now. Defer something if it can be done later and has no major consequences.

Do: If there is something necessary to do and you have the time to accomplish it, do it right away.

4. 18 minutes

The 18-minute strategy developed by Peter Bregman, CEO of global management consulting firm Bregman Partners, enables us to navigate through a tangle of emails, phone calls, text messages, and interminable meetings that hinder us from spending our time on what is important.

Five minutes in the morning: Sit down and consider what you need to do today to succeed. Then cross those items off your to-do list and add them to your calendar (use ProofHub's calendar).

Refocus for one minute per hour. Set an hourly alarm and when it goes off, "take a deep breath and ask yourself if you spent your last hour productively," he adds.

Turn off your computer for five minutes in the evening and reflect on your day.
Overall, the 18-minute strategy provides a simple way to organize your day and reclaim your life from distractions.
NOTE:

Time management is very crucial in our daily life. Gaining even a basic understanding of time management can have a profound impact on your life.Don't squander a minute of your precious time on things that won't make it better.

Time Management Strategies

Efficient time management is one of the most important keys to success, thus it is worthwhile to master. The following are time management strategies for employees and students to assist them manage their time as effectively as possible.

1. Plan Your Day Using a Daily Schedule Template

Seminars, lectures, and workshops may take up a portion of your day, but how you manage your personal time is crucial. It is critical to master your timetable.

A daily schedule template assists you in managing and controlling your time throughout the day. It will help you stay organized, focus on what is important, and even combat procrastination. Most successful people, from Elon Musk to Bill Gates, adopt the "time blocking" strategy. Time blocking is the process of developing a plan for how you intend to spend each minute of your day. Students should therefore use this strategy to better manage their time.

2. Recognize how you're currently spending your time (and where you're wasting it).

Your plan will provide you with an ideal version of your day, but in order to create better time management practices, you must assess how you spend your time. It is impossible to develop better time management tactics for students to stay focused until you understand how you spend your time each day.

3. Establish Specific Goals to Track Your Progress

Goals are a wonderful approach to push yourself to complete schoolwork. The problem is that objectives are simply the product of you not knowing how to achieve them. So, concentrate on what has to be done to attain that objective, such as making consistent improvement and building improved habits. Set a daily goal of 500 words if you need to produce a 5,000-word essay in a month, for example. If you keep doing this, you should be able to finish your essay in a week.

4. Divide large projects into smaller, more manageable tasks.

Separating huge goals from smaller daily activities is an important aspect of successful goal-setting. This will help you stay focused and prevent procrastination. When a project feels overwhelming, it is simple to delay. However, taking that first step is all that is required to gain momentum.

5. Be realistic about the amount of time required to complete a task.

When you start planning your day's chores, you may become excessively optimistic about how much you can accomplish. The Planning Fallacy is a term used by psychologists to describe this. Countering the planning fallacy is one of the most effective time management methods for students. Depending on how experienced they are with the assignment, students should add a buffer to their schedule. If it has been done before, 1-1.5X time must be assigned to the time they believe it will take to finish the job.

6. Be aware of your body's natural energy highs and lows.

We all have times during the day when we feel more energized and attentive. And if you want to make the most of the time you have each day, you can't battle your body's natural state. What does this signify in terms of student time management tips? Simply put, students should do their most important work while they are feeling the most energized. This involves arranging strenuous undertakings during high energy periods and passive activities during low energy periods.

7. Take Breaks at Appropriate Times

Increase your breaks to better manage your productivity over time. But when is it OK to take a break? According to sleep expert Nathaniel Kleitman, "our minds naturally crave breaks after every 90 minutes of intense work." Even if you don't have a timer set, your body will alert you to the need for a break by becoming sleepy, fidgety, hungry, or losing focus." When you start to feel this way, it's time to take a break.

8. Eliminate Distractions

There are numerous things that can divert kids' attention away from their schoolwork, including social media, cell phones, and pals. When it comes time to perform schoolwork, children must turn off their cell phones and log out of their social media accounts. Any time spent on schoolwork must be free of television and cell phones!

9. Stay away from multitasking.

When students' schedules are crowded, it may be tempting for them to believe they can multitask.

However, the more one tries to perform at once, the longer each task takes. Instead, studies have shown that intensely focusing on one activity at a time can increase productivity by up to 500%.

10. Establish Improved Routines and Habits for Long-Term Success

We are repeatedly who and what we do.One of the most effective time management tactics for students and everyone else is to build routines and habits that support the types of actions you want to perform more of, such as following a morning routine that focuses on getting an early win and preparing yourself for a productive day. Alternatively, set your goals and routines the night before to guarantee your nightly routine prepares you for an efficient following day.

Creating a Productive Attitude

Your attitude is everything. It is the foundation for all of your success and accomplishments in life. What you need to do is change your thinking. And if you want to achieve those objectives, you must adopt a productive attitude.

What exactly is a productivity mindset?

Many people believe they have a productive mindset or that they are productive, but they are simply busy. They are not completing activities and projects in a productive manner. A productive mentality implies that you are clear and focused on your goals and that you are using all of your own resources to attain those goals in an organized manner.

So, what are the traits of a productive mindset?

The following are the components of a productive mentality that you must nurture in order to succeed.

1. Inspiration

We are all aware that motivation is essential in achieving our objectives. We need something to pull us in the direction of the achievement we desire in life. And, while motivation can be fickle, it is critical in the early stages of developing a productivity mentality.

It will be difficult to be productive if you are not driven to complete tasks and cross items off your to-do list. There has been a lot of research done on the relationship between motivation and achievement. We recognize that whatever you want to do is fueled by a strong desire to succeed.

Establish specific motivations to help you get into a productive mentality. What are the internal or extrinsic motivators that drive you to succeed? Keep these reasons in mind and use them to help you get through your day productively.

2. Perseverance

Although motivation is a big component of getting you started on your objectives, you also need tenacity to keep going even when things go rough.

Sometimes your motivation isn't strong enough to get you through difficult times, especially when you don't feel like you're making any progress. Long-term success requires persistence and never giving up. Because it is unavoidable that you may face difficulties and hurdles in accomplishing your objectives.

Persistence is essential in overcoming any obstacle. Just keep plodding along, even if it's only a little bit each day. This mental attitude will fortify your resolve and enable you to be more productive.

3. Imagination

To make progress toward our objectives, we must first define those objectives. How can we build a strategy to get somewhere if we don't know where we're going?

Always have a mental picture of the life you want to create for yourself. That vision will guide you and assist you in being more productive throughout the day. Visualization is an excellent approach to keep on track with your vision. This is a highly effective approach used by athletes and top achievers to attain their objectives.

The power of visualization has been demonstrated to assist you in taking more action in your life and being more motivated to achieve your goals. If you want to be productive, you must have a clear vision. Maintain that vision and allow it to guide your activities at all times.

4. Attitude of Positivity

This is essential not only for a productivity attitude, but also for a success mindset in general. If you want to obtain any form of positive results in your life, you must maintain your positive attitude.

Your attitude influences how you live your life. And you have the ability to choose your attitude. Although it may appear that you have no influence over external conditions, you can always manage your attitude and how you feel about things. A optimistic outlook on life is absolutely necessary. It is required to be productive and to assist you in reaching your goals.

We all have unpleasant thoughts from time to time; it's a normal aspect of being human. However, the good news is that you may choose to transform those negative thoughts into positive ones. You have the option of not allowing negativity to govern your life. Maintain a positive attitude and actively concentrate on increasing your productivity to see what kind of outcomes you may get.

5. Establish A Routine

Routines are excellent for achieving a highly productive mental state. The phrase "routine" may sound dull and uninspiring to you, yet it is an essential component of planning a productive day.

Morning is the best time to create a routine. This will assist you in developing the necessary mindset to be productive. Create a habit that allows you to wake up your brain, feel motivated, and see your vision clearly.

6. Concentrate on One Thing

When you have a to-do list with multiple tasks on it, it is easy to become overwhelmed and feel unproductive. In fact, having too many tasks on your to-do list may make you less productive.

Concentrating on one task at a time can enhance your productivity significantly. Choose one task per day that you believe is critical for you to complete. If you finish that one task, you will feel accomplished.

Then, before you do anything else, set out to do that task. Don't let distractions derail you; instead, focus on one task at a time. Once you've completed that task, everything else you accomplish in your day is a bonus. This will give you a greater sense of accomplishment and will drive you to continue being productive.

7. Being mindful

Being mindful can also help you develop a productive mindset. Being totally aware of each moment might help you achieve mental clarity and calm.

Be present at all times during the day. What is it that you are working on, and why? Be focused and intentional about what you want to achieve. Every task you complete should contribute to your overall goal. If not, become more conscious of the goal you're aiming for and what has to be done to get there.

Concentration and Discipline Training

Discipline is crucial in today's fast-paced atmosphere for achieving our goals and reaching new heights of accomplishment. Discipline is the cornerstone for personal success and fulfillment, academic ambitions, and professional endeavors.

1. Establishing a Firm Foundation:

Discipline provides a solid foundation for us to build our lives on. By establishing regular routines, defining clear goals, and consistently adhering to them, we create a structure that supports our progress and personal advancement.

2.Time Management:

Discipline enables us to manage our time more effectively. It helps us prioritize tasks, eliminate distractions, and focus on what is truly important. By adopting rigorous time management, we may optimize productivity and make the most of every valuable moment.

3. Establishing Consistency:

Long-term success requires consistency. Discipline allows us to consistently show up, even when circumstances are difficult. By developing and adhering to regular habits, we promote resilience and increase our chances of success.

4. Developing Self-Control:

Discipline strengthens our self-control, helping us to resist momentary gratification and make decisions that align with our long-term goals. It helps to eliminate procrastination, build good habits, and avoid distractions that limit our progress.

5.Promoting Personal Growth:

Discipline motivates human development. It pushes us to step outside of our comfort zones, tackle new challenges, and gain new abilities. Through discipline, we widen our viewpoints, become lifelong learners, and reach our greatest potential.

6. Inspiring Others:

We inspire others by demonstrating discipline. Our commitment to discipline serves as a model for others to follow. Our acts can motivate and encourage our friends, family, and coworkers to create disciplined habits and pursue their goals with zeal.

Remember that discipline is about giving ourselves the tools we need to create the life we want, not about punishing or confining ourselves. We can cultivate discipline to attain success, fulfillment, and personal improvement.

CHAPTER 3 :

Making a List of Your Top Priorities

Every day at work, you're juggling a seemingly never-ending to-do list and attempting to fit in new tasks, but by the end of the week, you still don't feel like you've made a dent in your workload. Or maybe you have long-term ambitions for your job or career but don't seem to be getting any closer as time passes. Is this anything you've heard before?

It's not because you didn't try hard enough. In actuality, the average American currently works more than 40 hours per week, coming in at 41.5, with 11.1% working more than 50.

Overworking is also not a long-term solution to getting more done. It can actually exacerbate issues like job burnout (which affects more than half of the workforce), mental exhaustion, and increase the risk of heart disease and stroke. Because there are only so many hours in a day, making the most of them demands being ruthless about what you prioritize. We'll talk about how to successfully prioritize your duties in order to reduce stress and get more done in less time in this blog post.

What is the definition of task prioritization?

What is the definition of task prioritization? The practice of organizing your to-do list in order of importance in order to better manage how you spend your time is known as task prioritization. And, contrary to popular belief, 82% of people do not use a time management system at all!

When everything on your to-do list feels important, it might be tough to decide how to spend your limited time. This can lead to decision paralysis, which occurs when you are physically too burdened by your duties to begin. Alternatively, you may try to work on multiple 'important' tasks at the same time, which will result in a lot of context switching and would cost you 6 hours each day - as well as significantly lowering the quality of your work.

While it may appear that all of your responsibilities are equally important, this is not the case. At this stage, task prioritization becomes one of your most important productivity strategies. And the benefits are self-evident.

The following are the benefits of prioritizing your chores:

Stress is reduced since you know what to prioritize first.

Increases productivity by allowing you to concentrate on one high-priority task at a time.

Reduces context switching, which increases work quality.

Reduces decision paralysis, which prevents procrastination.

Positive outcomes and reduced stress boost motivation.

So, how do you manage all of your priorities, responsibilities, and deadlines? Let's talk about how to prioritize your work to boost your productivity.

Work Task Prioritization

1. Establish your goals.

How do you prioritize your weekly responsibilities if you don't know what your objectives are? Finally, rather of getting caught up in the whirling to-do list of the present, you should spend the majority of your time making progress on your most important goals.

That means the first stage is to review (or create) your short- and long-term goals, ensuring they are SMART goals to increase your chances of success. This can help you prioritize your ever-changing task list, stay motivated, and allocate your time to activities that will move you closer to your goals. It also makes you more conscious of the distractions that impede your development.

2. Make a task list.

It's not blissful ignorance when it comes to productivity.When you're pulling to-dos from your inbox, odd sticky notes, stray papers, and your project management tool as you go, it's all too easy to become disorganized - you just don't have a clear overview of all you need to do.

Make a comprehensive list of all of your chores to begin. Put all of your to-dos, projects, and requests in one digital list that you can easily review and edit later. Some popular project management applications are ClickUp, Todoist, and Asana, which may help you organize your task list and goal planning in one location. While it may feel overwhelming at first, and you will definitely have a long list, this phase is crucial because you need a comprehensive picture of all that needs to be done in order to build a realistic strategy that is aligned with your goals.

3. Sort by priority vs. urgency

So, where do you begin? It's time to prioritize your tasks now that you've gathered them all in one place. The Pareto Principle states that 80% of results come from 20% of the work, meaning that high-value tasks are more important because they provide higher returns toward your goals when completed. Tools like the Eisenhower Matrix can help you prioritize your master list when you're managing a task list that comprises both high-value and low-value activities.

Prioritizing initiatives includes balancing their importance and urgency. The Eisenhower Matrix, created by former US President Dwight Eisenhower, is a popular method for discriminating between 'urgent' and 'important' duties, especially when they all appear significant.

When using the Eisenhower Matrix to arrange your work list, divide your jobs into four groups:

. Urgent and critical tasks: Prioritize these chores over others.

Important but not critical: Make a plan to complete these tasks and set aside time to focus on them for long-term and strategic growth.

Delegate these chores to someone else or automate the process using smart solutions such as task prioritizing software if they are urgent but not important.

Remove these items from your agenda because they are neither urgent nor important.

Be critical of each task as well. You will not benefit from defining everything as critical when it is not. Your weekly time is limited, and you want your efforts to yield the best outcomes for you and your team.

4. Make time in your schedule

Determine your priorities first, and then make time to focus on them. Time blocking is a method of 'blocking' time in your calendar for certain tasks, in addition to all of your regular weekly meetings and appointments. And, by declaring your availability publicly, you not only make it easier to manage your workweek, but you also safeguard your time from being flooded with other people's priorities.

Setting daily goals and scheduling time for them in your calendar is the greatest method to ensure you have time to work on your important chores. You can also save time by planning out your week ahead of time, especially if you have a lot of meetings. You may also use a productivity app like Reclaim.ai to automatically sync your task list to Google Calendar and find the best time to work on your projects, routines, breaks, and even 1:1 meetings between two busy calendars.

5. Politely decline unimportant tasks

Important activities, according to the Eisenhower Matrix, are high-value to-dos that match with your goals, whereas urgent tasks are those that require immediate action, such as a project deadline that has been pushed up or a technical emergency. However, just because something is urgent does not always imply that it is important (as many of us are trained to believe).

Even if you've worked hard to prioritize your week, it's vital to remember not to leave your key responsibilities for every unexpected emergency. This includes saying no to another unnecessary meeting that might have been handled via email, or telling a coworker that you can't take on a last-minute request because you have important deep work to prioritize. Learning to properly say "no" to things for which you don't have the time or bandwidth is crucial for making meaningful progress on your goals.

6. Examine your time management and performance.

Have you ever been surprised by how little you accomplished on your to-do list by the end of the week? We are not always as productive as we think. In reality, 41% of activities are never completed, despite the fact that just 20% of people do time audits to check their productivity. A weekly or monthly audit of your calendar will help you understand where you're allocating your time, whether you were sidetracked by crises or overestimated the time it would take to accomplish a task.

Once you've recognized where your time is going, you can evaluate if your current time management technique is actually devoted to what's most important to you - and, most importantly, take action to correct it. You may realize that you spend half of your time in meetings, leaving you with less than 20 hours per week to concentrate on your responsibilities; hence, it may make sense to schedule a no-meeting day in the future to ensure more task time.

If completing a time audit manually sounds like too much work, you may automate the process by scanning your schedule and revealing where you're spending your time. Every Friday, all Reclaim users receive an email containing a weekly report indicating how much time was spent on task work vs. meetings vs. habits - making calendar audits as easy as checking your mailbox.

"Increased productivity equals improved task prioritization."

There are several tools and tactics for raising your weekly productivity, but focusing on your task prioritization skills is the most effective way to ensure that you are truly making the most of your important time.

You may build a plan around the things that are most important to you by establishing your goals and ruthlessly prioritizing your task list by priority vs. urgency, and begin saying no to the non-priorities that consume your workweek.

The Art of Dealing with What Really Matters

Because every person's life is unique, there can't be a single path that applies to everyone. Instead, here are three broad, structural methods to dealing with life. It is up to each of us to extract tactics that are personally relevant from them.

. Build up your experience. Life gives us experiences that assist us develop ways for dealing with potential issues. Throughout our lives, we modify these strategies: we fail, are ashamed or unfortunate, and attempt to fail better the following time - until we succeed or turn away. Even the most harrowing events can be used to better understand ourselves and the world. We may not want them, but it is up to each of us to put them to use.

Experiences occur all the time and do not require a particular location. They occur when we meet new people, read books, or watch movies. They don't even require outside input because our minds may generate them based on prior experiences, through thinking and introspection. They can also occur in our dreams, where our subconscious processes earlier occurrences. Life is continually revealing new things to us, and contemplation can occur anywhere - in front of an earlier work of yours, or during your everyday commute. Gather and apply your experiences to make sense of life.

. **Make new pals.** Life normally begins with a small group of trustworthy family members. We gradually broaden our social circle: kindergarten, school, and hobbies, employment, and university. Along the process, we meet like-minded people who provide a safe sanctuary for self-doubt, truth searches, and progress. They assist us in making sense of our experiences, developing plans, and dealing with forthcoming obstacles. We reciprocate by assisting them in making sense of their life. Some friends become colleagues in our professional initiatives, while others listen from afar; some are in our lives only momentarily, while others are there continuously - but all are significant. While some of us have ongoing inner dialogues to reflect on our experiences, others require external stimuli, such as other people. In any case, we need people to help us make sense of life.

. **Accumulate self-awareness.** As we become older, we have a better grasp of ourselves and our sensitivity, as well as a better understanding of our limitations and shortcomings. It's becoming increasingly clear who gives us good counsel and who harms us. Sometimes we put our trust in the wrong people and need to re-calibrate our internal compasses. Sometimes we employ the incorrect techniques. We notice patterns of ineffective conduct in both others and ourselves. Some can be overcome by reflection and hard work, while others benefit from psychotherapy's structural approaches. The greater our investment in self-awareness, the better we will comprehend ourselves, the world, and our place in it. The less we care, the harsher life becomes: gather and expand your self-awareness to make meaning of existence.

Our acts, no matter how hard we strive, are always ultimately insufficient; we can't know everything, and we can't "win" life. We all die eventually, and that's the end of it. Experience, friends, and self-awareness cannot protect us from this, but they can improve our lives. They will help us be more equipped for life and make us feel more welcome, and so constitute the ultimate aids. They keep us from always beginning over, which appears to be necessary in order to leave a constructive mark on the world.

CHAPTER 4:

Overcoming Procrastination

Do you have a problem with procrastination? Do you frequently procrastinate on crucial activities and struggle to meet deadlines?If this describes you, you are not alone.

Procrastination is a widespread issue that can afflict everyone, regardless of age, occupation, or background. Procrastination, on the other hand, does not have to be a permanent impediment to productivity. You can fight procrastination and increase your productivity with a few basic ideas and techniques. In this blog post, we'll look at some practical strategies and techniques for overcoming procrastination and achieving your goals. These tactics can help you take charge of your time and achieve your goals, whether you're a student, a professional, or anybody else trying to enhance your productivity. So let's get started on overcoming procrastination right away!

Many people deal with procrastination, which may be a huge impediment to reaching our objectives and being productive. We may, however, overcome procrastination and increase productivity with a few basic ideas and techniques. In this blog post, we'll look at several successful methods for overcoming procrastination and increasing productivity.

. Determine the source of your procrastination:

The first step toward overcoming procrastination is determining why you procrastinate. Does your current task seem too much for you?Do you lack motivation or concentration? Are you scared of failing? When you understand why you procrastinate, you can take actions to address the underlying problem.

. Divide the project into smaller, more achievable steps:

One of the most prevalent causes of procrastination is feeling overwhelmed by the size or intricacy of a task. To get around this, try breaking down the process into smaller, more doable steps. This can give you a sense of control and make the process appear less onerous. To track your progress and keep organized, you can also use a tool like a to-do list or a project management app.

. Set measurable objectives:

Setting concise, attainable goals might assist you in remaining focused and motivated. When making goals, keep the acronym SMART in mind: Specific, Measurable, Achievable, Relevant, and Time-bound. This will assist you in being accountable and tracking your progress toward your objective.

. Remove all distractions:

Distractions can be a major impediment to work. Try working in a quiet setting, turning off your phone, or using a website blocker to prevent yourself from visiting distracting websites to eliminate distractions. You can also attempt the Pomodoro Technique, which entails working in 25-minute bursts with short pauses in between.

. Determine accountability:

Being held accountable by someone can be a very powerful incentive. To stay on track and achieve your goals, you can locate an accountability partner, join a group or class, or hire a coach.

Reward yourself as follows:

Rewards can be an excellent method to keep employees motivated and productive. Take time to celebrate your accomplishments when you complete a task or reach a goal. Treat oneself to a favorite hobby, meal, or enjoyable outing. This will assist you in associating production with happy sensations, resulting in a positive feedback loop.

To summarize, procrastination can be a substantial impediment to productivity, but it is manageable with the correct strategies and techniques. You may increase your productivity and fulfill your goals by recognizing the core cause of procrastination, reducing activities into smaller pieces, defining precise goals, minimizing distractions, finding accountability, and rewarding yourself.

Stopping the Clock

We may enjoy doing our work, but when the pressure is on, we end up scrambling to complete it. Our deadlines begin to loom, and there is always the risk that we will fail to deliver on time. Here are 9 pointers to help you reach those unattainable deadlines.

1. Express yourself

Clearly define the level of quality you will provide in the time allotted. It is critical to express this before you and your customer commit to one other. You will be able to take charge of your timeline, operate more efficiently, and produce what you can and what the client requires by the deadline if you do this. Knowing the exact needs of your task will allow you to correctly plan out the steps you need to follow and the time required to complete each stage.

2. Avoid overcommitment

If you offer too much in an excessive length of time, you will not produce great outcomes. Before making any commitments, it is critical to understand exactly what you are capable of doing in the time frame agreed upon.

3. Establish Timetables

Track the progress you should make by scheduling important success elements and when they should occur in order to meet your deadline.

4. Allocate Enough Time

If the time allocated is not reasonable, you will never complete all of your task before the deadline. Before settling on a deadline, plan out the time required to complete your work. It is also critical to set aside enough time in your schedule to complete the assignment.

5. Schedule Buffers for Your Deadline

Do not aim solely for the deadline. To create room for unexpected outcomes and circumstances, try cushioning it by striving to accomplish the project before the deadline.

6. Maintain Concentration

Maintain your focus on your work. Make a point of giving your complete attention to the subject at hand, no matter how challenging it may be-here are some recommendations to help you stay focused (insert link to another blog post).

7. Concentrate on one task at a time

Concentrate on the work that has a tight deadline. You will be able to provide your full effort to your work if you focus all of your attention on one task. When you're rushed for time, multitasking may seem like a good idea, but lowering the quality of your work isn't a good alternative when it comes to maintaining a great work standard.

8. Do not accept new projects on which you are unable to work.

When you're up against an impossible deadline, stay focused and don't take on any new assignments. As appealing as it may seem, it may jeopardize the quality of your output and even your capacity to complete your assignment on time.

9. Get Enough Sleep

Recharge both your mind and your body. If you don't, you might be squandering your time by working when you're tired and bunting out. Rest permits you to work more efficiently.

Deadlines are a part of the job, but they don't have to hold you back from doing your best work. Do not succumb to the strain. Use these 9 pointers to help you beat the clock the next time you try.

Maintaining Health and Energy

Do you wake up most mornings feeling sluggish? Do you now need to consume coffee in order to get through the day?

If this sounds familiar, it's time to develop an energy management plan instead of relying on band-aid solutions. Although it may be intimidating to begin, you'll be inspired to continue once you see the advantages of leading a happier, healthier, and more productive lifestyle.

What exactly is energy management?

Think of your energy as a limited resource, just like the money in your bank account. You have a set amount of money to spend at the beginning of the day. The quantity varies based on age, sleep patterns, stress level, health conditions, and way of life.

Even while you might not always be able to stop doing things that drain your energy, you can still take action to refuel.

To live a happier, healthier, and more productive life, use these seven strategies for increasing energy:

1. Consume nutritious foods.

A healthy, well-balanced diet is the cornerstone of happiness. But generally speaking, eating healthily is seen as a means of losing weight. According to the 2020 Dietary Guidelines for Americans, a balanced diet high in fruits and vegetables, lean protein, low-fat dairy, and whole grains is necessary for healthy energy. You are truly what you eat.

To get a range of nutrients that will sustain you throughout the day, eat a variety of foods from all food categories. Select fresh or frozen fruits and vegetables, with a focus on nutrient-dense dark, leafy greens and broccoli, as well as orange vegetables like sweet potatoes and carrots. There are many different types of fish and beans to choose from when looking for good sources of protein. Eat three ounces of whole-grain breads, rice, pasta, or cereals each day.

2. Sleep for seven or eight hours every night.

Making sleep a priority is one of the best strategies to get ready for a productive, energetic day. Major health disorders can be made worse by sleep deprivation, which can also negatively affect your motivation, attitude, and energy levels. Sleeping enough is a healthy habit that many people need to improve. What prevents the majority of adults from sleeping for seven or eight hours every night?

If you have difficulty falling asleep, record your sleep habits. Note how much sleep you get each night, what influences how much sleep you get or don't get, how rested and energized you feel during the day. Then, to enhance your quality of sleep, think about sleep strategies like establishing a calm and relaxing atmosphere, reducing light and noise, creating a bedtime routine, managing stress, and turning off electronics.

Whatever you choose to begin with, stick with it. Maintaining the same sleeping routine and techniques can help your body's natural alarm clock develop and improve the quality of your sleep. Increased sleep leads to improved physical and mental health, a lower risk of illness, and increased productivity.

3. Be in the company of upbeat people.

Spend more time with those who make you happy to be around them. You'll feel energized and uplifted when you connect with positive people who share your interests.

Conversely, people who you can't relate to, who have a pessimistic attitude, complain a lot, or make bad decisions will deplete your energy reserves. Choose your associates carefully.

To protect yourself and preserve your energy, you must establish limits and boundaries when you're around people who don't replenish your energy supplies.

4. Steer clear of excessive news.

One essential method to keep up with global events is to consume news. It could be entertaining, enlightening, and even inspirational.

Sadly, news reports of suffering are all too common. These tales have the power to warp your perception of reality and make you concentrate more on your worst fears than on the positive things in your immediate environment.

Although it's impossible to completely avoid these stories, make an effort to limit your exposure, particularly during trying times.

5. Take part in regular exercise.

Do you typically feel sleepy in the middle of the day? Have you ever grown weary of performing basic daily duties like cleaning or grocery shopping? A minimum of 150 minutes a week of moderate-intensity physical exercise is recommended for adults by the Department of Health and Human Services. This will NOT lower your energy account; on the contrary, it will increase it.

Your body functions more effectively during other physical tasks or activities when you exercise because it releases tension and stress, builds muscle, and increases endurance.

6. Engage in meaningful activity each day.

What piques your interest? Would you like to develop or impart your special talent to others? Do something you enjoy every day, even if it's just preparing a healthy supper or listening to your favorite music. You can use and reserve your energy in ways that will maximize your potential by putting effort into the things that are meaningful to you.

7. Have optimistic thoughts about other people.

Keeping a compassionate attitude is another way to save energy. One way to practice this kind of thinking is to pay kind attention. Try smiling and making eye contact with a stranger while imagining "I wish you well." Rather, this kind deed may prevent you from criticizing that person. It can be stressful to engage in this kind of negative internal dialogue where we judge others and then judge ourselves.

You will feel better with every step you take toward making this important investment in self-care.

To help you start paying more attention to self-care, consider these few simple tasks:

Keep an eye on your energy levels.

Throughout the day, gauge your energy "temperature" and give it a number between 1 and 10, with 10 representing your highest energy level. Take note of the little things in your day so you can identify the people or circumstances that affect you the most.

Make a few minor changes.

Once you've determined which people or situations are depleting your energy, think about what you should do next. Instead of taking on everything at once, choose a task that is important to you and set attainable objectives. For instance, rather than trying to do it all at once, pick one cupboard, closet, or drawer each week to clean out if chaos in your home is a significant source of daily stress. Once you're prepared, move on to your next objective.

Organize and rank your time.

Make a note of the times of day when you feel most energized. When you are feeling productive and energized, prioritize important tasks to see how you can take advantage of those opportunities.

Work-Life Harmony

IMPORTANT DATA

The goal of work-life balance is to strike a balance between your personal obligations, your activities that "top you up," and your responsibilities at work or school.

A good work-life balance enables you to carve out time for your family and yourself while still being content and productive at work.

It might be difficult to clearly separate your days into work and home time if you work from home or have a part-time job.

It is not a sign of weakness to ask for help and support if you are feeling stressed and overwhelmed at work or at home.

What exactly is work-life balance?

job-life balance refers to balancing the responsibilities of job with your home and family life. If you struggle with work-life balance, you may find yourself racing to manage several commitments, leaving you feeling as if you are doing nothing well.

Working long hours might make it more difficult to strike a healthy balance between work and personal life. Working long hours can have a negative influence on your health, make your job dangerous, increase your stress levels, and reduce your time for leisure activities.

A good work-life balance implies that you have (most of the time) harmony between the various parts of your life. Outside of work, you will have time to care for yourself and your family, as well as engage in recreational activities. Personal care, socialization, hobbies, and leisure can all contribute to your general well-being.

It is critical to prioritize wellbeing, which is frequently regarded as less important than paid labor or housework.

Who finds it hard to strike a balance between life and work?

Australians put up a lot of effort. You could be one of the 13% (more than 1 in 10) who work more than 50 hours every week. The Organization for Economic Cooperation and Development (OECD) considers this to be "very long hours."

Overtime is prevalent, especially if you are young, male, or work full-time.

If you have a family, you may be under pressure to do both:

. support them by working

. look after them at home by conducting chores

If you are studying as well as working, it may be more challenging to strike a decent balance in your life.

Many people perform part-time, low-wage, informal occupations that require them to work unsocial hours. When you have less employment than you need to support your bills and costs, your stress levels rise and your mental health suffers.

What are the advantages and disadvantages of working?

While not everyone can work, working generally improves your mental and physical health and well-being.

Work may include:

. give you a regular routine and structure

. increase your physical activity levels

. create a sense of belonging

. give your life meaning and purpose

. serve as a source of friendship

. supply you with a sense of approval

. provide you with financial independence

. Unemployment, on the other hand, can have a negative impact on both mental and physical health.

Working may have drawbacks that contribute to your stress levels. Here are several examples:

a sense of isolation or loneliness at work

. receiving little recognition for your work

Worrying about losing your work or not receiving enough shifts

a lack of control over one's job

If you are fatigued from working long hours or shift work, you may feel insecure at work.

. pressure to stay online over the weekend or check emails when on vacation

If you can strike a good balance between work and other obligations, you are more likely to:

. be more content

. to become more productive

. Taking fewer sick days

. keep your employment for a longer period of time

If your company allows it, flexible hours and working from home can be beneficial. You can inquire about flexible working arrangements with your company.

Burnout

Burnout occurs when you:

For a long time, feel mentally and physically fatigued, have a lack of interest in work, hate or avoid going to work, feel overwhelmed and emotionally drained, and find it difficult to execute simple everyday activities

Burnout can cause the following symptoms: physical symptoms such as stomach pains, headaches, and sleep disturbances make it difficult to concentrate or be creative lead to negative feelings about your coworkers and a lack of confidence in your own ability to function at work cause a lack of enthusiasm or drive to do your work well

Burnout can occur when you devote all of your energy to your work for an extended period of time while neglecting your health, family, and friends.

Burnout is a severe kind of work-related stress. It could also be because of other aspects of your life, such as being a long-term caregiver.

Tips for achieving a healthy work-life balance

1. Be aware of your values.

Take some time to consider what matters most to you in life. Consider your interests and passions, and make time for the activities that bring you joy. What's your time allocation for your top priorities?

2. Exercise time management skills.

Ever ponder how the day has flown by? Calendars, apps, and to-do lists are all effective tools for tracking how you spend your time.

You may go over a normal week and see if you can make better use of your time. You may be able to save time by doing more online shopping or working from home a couple of days a week to cut down on your commute. You may see if any meetings or responsibilities can be completed via phone, video, or email rather than in person.
You may notice that social media is consuming large portions of your day.

3. Establish limits

If you find it difficult to say no, you could consider limiting your work time and scheduling time for other activities ahead of time.

Inform others when you will be unavailable. Step away from your phone, turn off your work emails, or disconnect from the internet for a few hours.

Do you have somebody who can help you? Can you let go of the strain and accept that good enough is enough?

4. Have fun at work

'Do what you love and enjoy what you do,' is a terrific motto to live by and something to strive for. Most professions can be tedious or unpleasant at times, but if you truly despise your job or it is making your life difficult, it may be time for a change.

Inquire with your company about flexible working arrangements. Check to see if you can transfer to a new team or retrain. You may start a side hustle for a few hours per week to experiment with a different way of making a living.

5. Examine your financial situation

Do you truly require a new car or laptop? Could you get some of the items you require secondhand? Can you live in a smaller house? Can you 'DIY' some of your house renovation? Can you bring your lunch to work instead of ordering takeout?

Perhaps you are eligible for government assistance.

According to research, if our basic needs are addressed, a larger income does not always contribute to happiness. Spending less money could mean working fewer hours and having more time to yourself.

6. Foster relationships

Positive relationships and social support aid in the development of resilience and lead to more adaptable ways of dealing with stress. It takes time to nurture and create strong relationships.

Make time for your family, friends, neighbors, and loved ones.

7. Pay attention to your health.

Exercise has been shown to alleviate stress, anxiety, and depression.

Make sure you receive enough rest at regular intervals.

Eat healthful foods, use alcohol in moderation, and stay away from illegal narcotics.

8. Schedule downtime

It is critical to take time to rest and recharge in order to achieve in what is essential to you. Schedule regular time off each week for yourself to unwind, read a book, play a sport, spend time in nature, or simply do nothing. Select any activity that you enjoy.

CHAPTER 5:

Spreading the 5AM Club Principles in Your Organization

The Strength of a 5 AM Club-Aligned Team

1. Create a sense of shared accountability by introducing the 5 AM Club ideals to your team. When everyone commits to getting up early and making the most of their mornings, it becomes a team effort to meet personal and team objectives. Team morale and motivation can benefit from shared accountability.

2. Increased Productivity: Consider a complete team that begins each day with a disciplined morning routine centered on self-improvement and high-impact tasks. This shared dedication to productivity can result in improved team performance and output.

3. Developing a Growth Mindset: The 5 AM Club ideals emphasize the importance of constant self-improvement. When a group adopts this mindset, they become more open to learning and growth, which leads to innovation and flexibility.

4. Increased Team Bonding: The shared experience of getting up early and working together to achieve a common objective can help to enhance team relationships. As team members share their morning routines, goals, and progress, they become more connected.

Steps for Spreading the 5 AM Club Principles in Your Organization

1. Set a Good Example: In order to properly convey the 5 AM Club values to your team, you must set a good example. Share your personal morning routine, triumphs, and problems to demonstrate your dedication to these concepts.

2. Educate Your Team: Hold workshops or training sessions to teach your team to the 5 AM Club ideals. Explain the reasoning behind these ideas, emphasizing the advantages of starting the day early.

3. Establish clear and Measurable Goals: Encourage your staff to establish clear and measurable goals for their morning routines. Having clear objectives, whether it's reading for 30 minutes, exercising, or focusing on a specific project, helps boost motivation.

4. Morning Huddles: Implement morning huddles or stand-up meetings in which team members share their morning successes, challenges, and goals. This technique not only fosters accountability, but it also allows team members to encourage one another.

5. Develop a Morning Ritual: Create a morning ritual that is unique to your team or organization. A morning mantra, team affirmations, or a shared team activity that sets a positive tone for the day can all be included.

6. Provide Resources: Provide resources and tools to assist your team in putting the 5 AM Club ideas into action. This could involve suggesting books, applications, or online courses related to personal development and productivity.

7. input and Adaptation: Gather input from your team on a regular basis to understand what is working and what needs to be improved. Adapt your strategy based on their feedback to maintain their enthusiasm.

8. Recognize and honor team members who consistently embrace the 5 AM Club ideals and show remarkable commitment and results. Positive encouragement can help to keep the practice going.

Overcoming Obstacles

Spreading the 5 AM Club values in your company can be extremely profitable, but it is not without difficulties. Here are some common roadblocks and solutions:

1. Reluctance to Change: Some team members may be reluctant to get up early. To combat this, emphasize the positives and provide assistance in making the change.

2. Sustainability: Early morning routines might be difficult to maintain. Encourage your staff to start small and progressively increase their wake-up time to 5 a.m.

3. Distinct Circadian Rhythms: Everyone's body clock is unique. Recognize that not all team members will be productive at 5 a.m. Allow for some leeway in the time of morning routines.

4. other circumstances: Life events and other circumstances might cause morning habits to be disrupted. When disruptions arise, encourage your team to adapt and not be too hard on themselves.

5. Maintaining Enthusiasm: To keep the enthusiasm going, revisit the benefits of the 5 AM Club on a regular basis and celebrate team triumphs.

Study of Cases

Let's look at a few of case studies to demonstrate the effectiveness of adopting the 5 AM Club concepts within a team or business.

Case 1: Tech Startup "Early Innovators"

Background: "Early Innovators" is a digital business that opted to follow Robin Sharma's 5 AM Club ideas after reading his book. These principles were incorporated into the company culture.

The organization claimed a considerable boost in productivity within a year. Members of their team were more focused, innovative, and goal-oriented. The shared commitment to the 5 AM Club principles increased teamwork and collaboration as well.

Case Study 2: The Nonprofit "Dawn of Change"

The nonprofit group **"Dawn of Change"** works on social and environmental issues. They introduced the 5 AM Club ideas to their personnel in order to increase efficiency and personal development.

The organization noticed a significant improvement in team morale and excitement. Team members began their days with a renewed feeling of purpose and were better prepared to face their cause's obstacles. This resulted in increased donor engagement and improved project outcomes.

Spreading the 5 AM Club ideals among your team members is an effective method to tap into the collective potential of early risers. Your team may achieve more success and pleasure by fostering a culture of accountability, productivity, and personal growth. While fully integrating these ideas into your team's routine may take some time, the long-term advantages are well worth the effort. Keep in mind that the road to becoming a 5 AM Club team is just as essential as the destination, and the transformation that occurs along the way can be absolutely astounding.

Stories of Success

The 5 AM Club's life lessons are exactly the learning and inspiration you need to confront your complacency. You might not have time to read this fantastic book if you're in a hurry. So, for your convenience, we've summarized the essential book takeaways.

1. The zeal of getting up early

This is the book's most important piece of advise to everyone. Getting up at 5 a.m. every day can do wonders for avoiding failure and making achievement a natural habit. We have more time than others when we wake up at 5 a.m. Furthermore, this is when we have the fewest interruptions and the most mental power.

In addition, the tranquility of early morning is priceless! You should plan your most critical chores for the day between 5 and 8 a.m. This book explains in simple terms how we can train and improve our minds to be more productive by waking up early. This vitality you have when you wake up in the morning, as well as the few extra hours in your day, are the right components for success.

"The secret to productivity is simplicity."

2. The ability to strike the correct balance in life

The book discusses a valuable lesson on achieving the perfect balance within. We frequently discuss the importance of mindfulness and developing the proper mentality to view things. But this book goes a step further than our ordinary attitude to life. It emphasizes the importance of mentality and introduces the terms heartset, healthset, and soulset.

These terms may appear unfamiliar, but they are self-explanatory. The concept of heartset supports the importance of emotional stability and well-being. Following that, the healthset perspective emphasizes the importance of maintaining physical health. Finally, soulset is a spiritual quality. As shown in this book, striking the appropriate balance between these internal characteristics can significantly improve one's chances of success.

3. The well-known 20/20/20 mode of operation

What will you do first if you begin waking up at 5 a.m. every day? Did you ever give it any thought? This book offers the solution, and you will be convinced that it is a fantastic way to start your day!. The author recommends dividing the first hour of the day into three equal halves of 20 minutes each.

Prioritize your physical health and exercise in the first 20 minutes of the day. You should spend the next 20 minutes recharging your soul and spirit via self-reflection and soulful meditation. This will help you prepare for the rest of the day and increase your devotion and focus. You should read and learn for the remaining 20 minutes of the first hour. But what exactly are you going to read in those 20 minutes? Read about successful people and their inspirational journeys to the top.

4. The importance of a regular sleep pattern

There is a reference of 'a vicious worldwide sleep recession' in this book, which is both intriguing and illuminating. It alludes to the state of sleep deprivation that this world is increasingly sliding into. We frequently link achievement and hard work with staying up all night and pushing our stamina to its limits. However, this is not the correct technique to achieving success, or rather, it is a defective methodology.

Even when we don't have any important work to complete, we may spend our evenings on social media or watching television. The true question is what we gain from it, and I'm afraid the answer is nothing! This book teaches us that it is vital to maintain your sleep cycle and begin your day at 5 a.m. sharp. Sleep and rest are essential for mental and physical well-being; otherwise, your productivity will suffer.

Still, you must be willing to do and suppose like only 5 do and suppose," If you want to have the results only 5 have."

5. The Evolutionary Art

The book emphasizes the need of becoming spiritual and mastering self-reflection. However, do you grasp the significance of your early reflection routine? The objective is to keep learning, reflecting on mistakes, and evolving as a continuous process. Every day, you should change and aspire to be a better version of yourself. As a result, one of your first priorities after waking up should be to reflect on your previous day's activities and missed chances.

To summarize, The 5 AM Club is a must-read novel for any avid reader. It has the ability and charm to completely change your perspective on life. Even if you are unable to read the book for any reason, make sure you apply the essential points listed above into your life. You can reclaim your lost soul and excitement by starting your day at 5 a.m., and you won't be able to moan about a lack of time. If you can own your mornings, you can go up the success ladder, because excuses are only used by those who are not devoted to their goals.

Observing Time Masters

Knowing how to prioritize your coursework is a critical skill on your way to effectively graduating from a distance learning program if you plan to follow the less traveled road and seek an online Master's degree.

You will have to choose when to read, research, and study. You must determine the optimum time for you to get courses and instruction. Without any actual structure, you, the future online student, will be forced to devise your own schedule and workflow.

Whatever online course and university you choose, you will need these essential time management and study/work schedule suggestions.

1. Make a schedule for your studies.

Create a clear timetable for yourself, with specified time intervals that are purely committed to taking your classes and going through online tutorials, as one strategy to manage your future online study programme.

Instead of trying to accommodate your online courses around your life and hobbies, do the opposite. Arrange your hobbies to complement your academics. It will give you the impression that you are enrolled as a student in a typical classroom and will demonstrate your dedication to your studies.

The fundamental distinction is that this schedule is created by you rather than enforced by the institution. So, if it's more convenient for you to study at night, after you've returned home from your full-time job, and just work twice a week, you have the freedom and flexibility to do so.

Simply choose the optimum time to fit your schoolwork into your schedule. However, with this much leeway, it is simple to lose track of your studies. That is why having a rigorous, solid framework to your working hours will assist you in avoiding the urge to postpone and squander time.

2. Maintain your discipline and motivation.

When you become a distance learning student, you will discover that it can be tough to encourage oneself to do your work, especially when there is no one looking over your shoulder to ensure that it is done. This is true whether you pursue a Bachelor's, Master's, or even a Ph.D.

Self-discipline and self-motivation are among the most difficult talents to cultivate in your life, but there are a few approaches that will effectively lead to good study habits.

As with many duties, chores, and projects, creating small incentives, or rewards, for yourself will make you feel extra motivated to finish your work.

When you finish your work, reward yourself with a dessert or tell your buddies, "I can't hang out with you until I finish my online tutorial." Set a deadline for yourself and tell yourself, 'If I finish this by 2:00, I will go get a cup of coffee.'

Incentives, both large and small, are a terrific way to give yourself that extra push, that extra piece of drive to do all of your job on your own. You'll want to find strategies to persuade you to sit down, log on, and work without being tempted to do anything else, especially if you're taking online classes.

3. Establish deadlines for all assignments, large and small.

You probably have the practice of performing your assignments one after the other, based on deadlines; that is, you will begin with the assignments that are due first, and then go on to the ones that are due later. While this may appear to be a clever strategy to complete your homework, it is not the most effective way to work.

Instead, think about how much work and time your assignments will require, and start with the most difficult ones. For example, if you've been given an online quiz, a 10-page paper, and a group project, you should probably start with the group project first, even if it's not the most important work.

Consider that group assignments can be especially tough to manage as an online student. Your classmates may live in different areas and have different commitments, and you may be required to meet via Skype at times. Planning and organizing a meeting with all of your virtual students will take far more time than, say, prepping for a brief quiz.

So, instead of putting off the harder tasks until last, begin with them while keeping a careful eye on your deadlines. This is a beneficial method of time management that is both practical and efficient and does not require you to squeeze everything into a short schedule.

Conclusion

Adopting the 5 a.m. Lifestyle for Business Success

The pursuit of excellence is an ongoing endeavor in the realm of business and professional accomplishment. To excel, one must not only be well-versed in information and skills, but also be skilled in time management, productivity, and personal development. The 5 AM lifestyle has evolved as a significant and revolutionary method to obtaining success in the corporate world within this sector. As we near the end of our investigation into this lifestyle and its consequences for business, it becomes clear that rising up at 5 a.m. is more than just a habit—it's a mindset, a philosophy, and a catalyst for success.

5 a.m. Lifestyle Recap

Before we get into the last remarks, let's go over the fundamentals of the 5 AM lifestyle. This way of living, popularized by Robin Sharma's book "The 5 AM Club," entails getting up at 5 a.m. and devoting the first hours of the day to personal development, physical wellness, and concentrated work. It is a dedication to prioritizing oneself, both intellectually and physically, in order to obtain an advantage in a world filled with competition and obstacles.

The 5 AM lifestyle revolves around four fundamental components:

1. The Victory Hour: This is the first hour of the day, usually between 5 and 6 a.m., when people engage in activities that improve their thinking, health, and productivity. It could involve things like meditation, exercise, journaling, reading, and goal-setting.

2. The 20/20/20 Formula: As part of the Victory Hour, this formula advises breaking the hour into three 20-minute segments for concentrated focus. The first 20 minutes are for exercise, the following 20 minutes are for introspection and self-improvement, and the final 20 minutes are for day planning and strategy.

3. Elite Performance's Twin Cycles: The 5 AM lifestyle highlights the importance of ultradian rhythms, which are 90-120 minute cycles during which our energy and focus peak. Individuals can improve their work and productivity by adhering to these cycles.

The importance of conquering the four interior empires—Mindset, Heartset, Healthset, and Soulset—is also highlighted by the 5 AM lifestyle. These characteristics indicate an individual's entire development and are necessary for success and fulfillment.

The Road to Business Success

Adopting the 5 AM lifestyle has enormous possibilities for anyone seeking commercial success. This is why:

1. Increased Productivity: Waking up at 5 a.m. allows for an uninterrupted, distraction-free atmosphere. This golden time can be directed toward high-impact tasks, resulting in enhanced productivity and higher work quality. It sets the tone for a productive and focused workday.

2. Personal Growth and Development: The 5 AM lifestyle stresses personal development. Successful business executives and entrepreneurs recognize that professional success is inextricably linked to personal development. The Victory Hour promotes the development of new abilities, self-awareness, and a growth mentality.

3. Better Time Management: Adopting a disciplined morning routine helps an individual align their objectives and goals. This, in turn, improves time management abilities. Knowing that the early morning hours are dedicated to personal development and work ensures that critical chores be done promptly.

4. Stress Reduction: The peace and quiet of early mornings can help to reduce stress levels dramatically. Individuals who engage in activities that enhance mental and physical well-being are better prepared to deal with the unavoidable obstacles and pressures of the corporate world.

5. Competitive Advantage: Having a competitive advantage is critical in today's competitive business world. Individuals benefit from the 5 a.m. lifestyle. Individuals can distinguish themselves in their particular industries by committing to personal and professional development on a constant basis.

6. Leadership and Influence: Those who embrace the 5 a.m. lifestyle frequently find themselves in positions of leadership. By setting a good example, they can persuade their teams and companies to follow suit. The influence of a leader who practices the 5 AM lifestyle might result in cultural shifts within organizations.

7. Fulfillment and Balance: Business success is about more than just monetary gains or professional achievements. The 5 a.m. lifestyle promotes life balance. Individuals can discover a great sense of fulfillment and contentment by devoting time to personal well-being, relationships, and self-improvement.

Last Thoughts

Adopting the 5 AM lifestyle for business success is a journey of dedication and development. It is a road that necessitates discipline, constancy, and tenacity. The discipline of rising at 5 a.m. is about more than just beating the clock; it is also about mastering oneself.

We've witnessed the dramatic influence the 5 AM lifestyle can have on individuals and, by extension, their business pursuits in this investigation. It is a way of life that promotes the ideals of discipline, ambition, and personal development, all of which are necessary for success in today's fast-paced corporate world.

Finally, it's critical to understand that embracing the 5 AM lifestyle is not a one-size-fits-all answer. What works for one person may not work for another, which is absolutely OK. The idea is to personalize the 5 AM lifestyle concepts and practices to your specific goals, circumstances, and tastes.

Whether you choose to get up at 5 a.m., 6 a.m., or 7 a.m., the essential ideas of self-improvement, mindfulness, productivity, and holistic growth are still relevant. The essence of the 5 AM lifestyle is making a conscious decision to invest in your personal and professional development.

Finally, the 5 AM lifestyle is a call to action—a call to seize charge of your life, time, and destiny. It serves as a reminder that corporate success does not begin with external circumstances, but rather with mastering the internal impulses that drive us. Accepting the 5 AM lifestyle is a step toward personal and professional success, and it is proof of the enduring force of human drive, perseverance, and the quest of perfection.